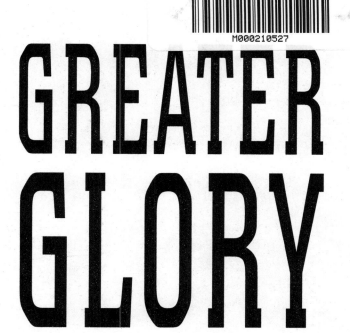

GREATER GLORY

GREATER GLORY

KENNETH E. HAGIN

22 21 20 19 18 17 16   11 10 09 08 07 06 05

Greater Glory
ISBN-13: 978-0-89276-529-4
ISBN-10: 0-89276-529-1

In the U.S. write:
Kenneth Hagin Ministries
P.O. Box 50126
Tulsa, OK 74150-0126
1-888-28-FAITH
rhema.org

In Canada write:
Kenneth Hagin Ministries of Canada
P.O. Box 335, Station D
Etobicoke (Toronto), Ontario
Canada M9A 4X3
1-866-70-RHEMA
rhemacanada.org

Contents

Preface

The Thursday before *Campmeeting 1987* began, I woke up in the night and began to pray. I prayed in other tongues for more than three hours. At the end of that time in prayer, I had a vision in which I saw the Tulsa Convention Center, where we hold our annual *campmeeting*. In the vision, Jesus and I were standing near the ceiling of the building, looking down on one of the *Campmeeting* services. The auditorium was full of people, and everyone was clapping. Then Jesus turned to me and said, "Clapping is neither praise nor worship."

Well, that startled me for moment. So He went on to explain: "Clapping is *applause*."

Then He illustrated it to me saying, in effect, "If clapping were praise or worship, then people at political rallies are praising and worshipping God when they clap. And if clapping were praise or worship, then people at ball games are also praising and worshipping God when they clap. You shouldn't clap for God; you should *reverence* Him."

Then the Lord said to me, "You've gone as far as you can go [spiritually] under the present circumstances. Tell My people to quit clapping and start praising. Then they will move up to a greater glory."

The way we will move into God's greater glory is through reverencing the Lord. As we learn to reverence Him, we must learn when to clap and when not to clap. You see, sometimes clapping is fine, but when it is inappropriate, it grieves the Holy Spirit. And if we grieve the Holy Spirit, we can't move into the greater glory.

Therefore, it is vitally important that we learn to flow with the Holy Spirit and return to true praise and worship. When we learn to praise God the right way, we will experience a deeper move of the Holy Spirit in our midst.

I pray that this book will help believers understand the difference between clapping and praising and reveal the importance of reverencing God as we learn how to walk in the greater glory.

Praising God Is the Key to Victory!

Over the years I have taught a lot on the subject of prayer. When the Lord directed me to begin holding Holy Ghost Meetings, He told me to teach on the subject of prayer in the day services and to teach it by precept and example. I *have* done that, I *am* doing that, and I *will continue* to do that. I want to share with you some truths about prayer. Let's start by looking at Acts 16.

> **ACTS 16:25**
> 25 And at midnight Paul and Silas prayed, and sang praises unto God: and the prisoners heard them.

I believe that the phrase "at midnight" was actually referring to the midnight hour. But, on the other hand, I believe that the word "midnight" can also be used figuratively. The midnight hour is sometimes the darkest hour in your life—in your greatest test or trial in which it seems there's no way out.

You see, Paul and Silas had been whipped and their backs were bleeding. They had been put in the innermost prison with their feet in stocks. They were in a most uncomfortable position. But, thank God, this text tells you what to do at midnight.

The psalmist of old said, *"The entrance of thy words giveth light"* (Ps. 119:130). So it may be a midnight hour in your life, but you're enlightened because the Word tells you what to do. Do just what Paul and Silas did. At midnight they prayed *and* sang praises unto God, and the prisoners heard them. That means they were praying and singing praises out loud at midnight!

Well, thank God, not only did the prisoners hear them, but God heard them. He reached down and shook that old jail until every door flew open and the stocks fell off the prisoners' feet. The jailer thought the prisoners had all escaped, and he knew that his superiors would kill him if they had, so he was going to fall on his sword and kill himself.

But Paul said, "Do thyself no harm; we're all here." The jailer called for a light, sprang in, and said to Paul and Silas, "Sirs, what must I do to be saved?" And he was saved, glory to God (Acts 16:26–32)!

Now this is the thought that I want to get over to you: The answer came while Paul and Silas were *praising* God, not while they were *praying*. Prayer is important, and prayer has its place. But prayer alone won't get the job done. That may surprise you, but it's absolutely true. Prayer alone didn't get the job done for Paul and Silas, did it?

No, the answer came while they were praising God. I believe that if people would quit praying over and over about the same thing and start praising God, it wouldn't be long until they'd have the answer and the victory.

The Answer Comes When You're Praising God

Many years ago—in March 1945 to be more exact—I was holding a meeting in Overton, Texas. The oil business was booming in those days. I was staying in the home of the pastor for whom I was holding the meeting. One day the pastor, his wife, and I went to eat the noon meal in the home of one of their parishioners.

We were sitting at the table talking, and the woman who had invited us for lunch said, "Brother Hagin, something happened to me about eight years ago, and I didn't understand it. But after hearing you teach and preach, I've come to understand some things."

She told me that she used to have asthma. Well, the largest city near Overton was Tyler, so she went to the doctor there. He had sent her to a doctor in Shreveport, Louisiana, and then finally to a world-renowned specialist in Dallas. She said, "My husband had a responsible position with one of the oil companies. He spent $10,000 on me and I was no better." Now you have to realize those were Depression Days and money wasn't worth what it is now. Ten thousand dollars doesn't sound like a lot of money, but it would be more like $150,000 today.

She continued, "Several ministers came along and held revivals in our church, and whenever anyone prayed for the sick, I'd get in the healing line. Even Brother Raymond T. Richey [a healing evangelist of that day] put his tent up here in East Texas. Well, I got a healing card and finally got in the healing line. He anointed me with oil and started to pray. Then he stopped and looked at me and said, 'You've been prayed for many, many times, haven't you?'"

"Oh, yes," she said.

Brother Richey said, "I'm not going to pray for you. Will you do what I tell you to do?"

She said, "I will, if it's easy." You see, everyone is looking for something easy.

He said, "Well, this is easy. Every time you think of it, just praise God for your healing."

"But I'm not healed yet," she said. In other words, she was saying, "How can I praise God for something I don't have? I'm not healed yet."

So Brother Richey said, "Can you praise God for the Word?"

"Oh, yes. I can praise God for the Word."

"Well," he said, "the Word says in Matthew 8:17 that Jesus 'took your infirmities and bare your sicknesses,' and First Peter 2:24 says, 'By His stripes, you were healed.'"

She said, "Yes, I know those scriptures are in the Bible."

Then Brother Richey said, "All right, then. Every time you think of it, just say, 'Thank You, Father, for the Word. According to the Word, I'm healed.' Can you do that?"

"Yes, I'll do it," she said.

Then the woman told me, "I got taken up with praising the Lord. I'd praise God while I was cooking breakfast and getting my husband off to work and the children off to school. I'd praise God while I was making up the beds and cleaning up the house. Every time I'd think of it, I'd praise God for the Word.

"I got to where I went to bed and woke up praising God for the Word. Then one day, I said to my husband 'You know it's been so long since I had an asthma attack,

I don't even remember the last attack I had.' My husband said, 'I do. It's been thirty days.'"

Then she said, "Brother Hagin, that thirty days has stretched into eight years, and I've never had another asthma attack!"

Now she had been prayed for again and again by every healing evangelist who came to minister in her local church. But the answer came when she began to praise God!

Here's another illustration of how praising God wins the victory. I heard Brother B_____'s testimony of healing back in 1937. Then in 1941, I had him hold a revival meeting in my church, and I personally asked him about his testimony. He was a young, single man in his late twenties or early thirties, and he met a lovely young lady in one of his meetings. They developed a relationship and got married. He was an evangelist and she was a wonderful singer, a marvelous complement to his ministry.

They preached constantly, holding revival meetings all over Texas, Oklahoma, New Mexico, Arkansas, and Louisiana. Then his doctor discovered that he had tuberculosis. Now if you go back and check the records, you'll find out that in the early 1930s, tuberculosis was about the number one cause of death in the United States.

Brother B_____ told me, "On the last night of every meeting that I conducted, I would tell the people that I had TB. Then I'd ask them to pray for me every time they thought of it."

Of course, everyone said they would pray for him every time they thought of it. Hundreds of people were praying for him. Even if they each prayed only a few minutes a day, if you put it all together, they got in hours of prayer for this brother. But he grew steadily worse. Finally, he just couldn't go anymore, so he went to his father-in-law's farm, about fifty miles south of Dallas, to die.

Brother B_____ was hemorrhaging in his lungs and had become bedfast. He told me, "I couldn't turn over in bed, I was so weak. I was near death. They had to turn me over on a sheet, but I could still move my head. One day, my father-in-law was out on the back side of the farm plowing, and my wife and mother-in-law were out behind the house doing the wash on those old-fashioned wash boards.

"I turned my head and looked out the window. I saw a clump of bushes and some trees about a quarter of a mile away from the house. And I don't know why, but I prayed, 'Father, if You'd just give me enough strength to get up and go down there to that clump of bushes and trees, I'll pray until I'm healed or dead, one of the two.'

"So I made an effort and managed to get up and make my way slowly down to those bushes. When I got there, I just gave out and fell on the ground. I didn't even have enough strength to whisper. I said to myself, 'When I get enough strength, I'm going to start praying, and I'm going to pray until I'm healed or I'm dead.'

"As I lay there, I began to think, 'If prayer alone was going to get it done, I'd already be healed, because hundreds of people have prayed.' So I changed. I said, 'I'm going to lie here and praise God until I'm healed or I'm dead.' It took all the strength I had just to whisper,

'Praise the Lord. Glory to God.' But at the end of two-and-one-half hours, I was standing on my feet hollering, 'Praise God!' so loudly that people heard me two miles away! And I've been healed ever since."

You see, the victory—the answer—came while he was praising God. Thank God for prayer. You must understand that I'm not belittling prayer. But can you see where we've missed it and come up short? The answer came for Paul and Silas, the woman with asthma, and Brother B_____ while they were praising God!

Give 'Equal Time' to Prayer and Praise

Most people do a lot of praying, but how much praising do they do? They're always asking God to do something, and, of course, that's scriptural. But it's when we spend equal time fellowshipping with the Lord in prayer and singing praises to Him that we see mighty manifestations of His power in our lives.

> **ACTS 16:25–26**
> **25 And at midnight Paul and Silas PRAYED, AND SANG PRAISES UNTO GOD: and the prisoners heard them.**
> **26 And suddenly there was a great earthquake, so that the foundations of the prison were shaken: and immediately all the doors were opened, and every one's bands were loosed.**

It's important to notice that Paul and Silas gave equal time to prayer and praise. Paul and Silas had already offered up a *prayer to God*, but their answer came when they offered up *praise to God!*

When I first came over in Pentecostal circles in 1937, I read a woman missionary's testimony of healing in a Pentecostal periodical. She had been healed of smallpox many years before the smallpox vaccine was developed.

When this woman got smallpox, her doctor isolated her, because smallpox is contagious. He didn't want it to spread. The woman said in her testimony that while she was in isolation, she began to pray and the Lord gave her a vision. In her vision, she saw an old-fashioned scale that balanced weight.

On one side it said "prayer"; it was full and sat down on the bottom. The other side said "praise," and there was just a little bit in it, so it hung in the air. Then the Lord spoke to her, saying, "When your praise equals your prayers, you'll be healed."

So for two days and nights, all she did was praise God, and she was completely healed! Every sign of smallpox just disappeared when her praises equaled her prayers.

Praising God Creates an Atmosphere for the Holy Spirit to Work In

We miss out on many of God's blessings because we don't take the time to get in the attitude of worship. I believe there is a close relationship between ministering to the Lord and receiving from Him. Praising God creates an atmosphere for the Holy Spirit to work in. When we learn to lift our voices in praise to the Lord, His supernatural power will begin to manifest in our lives!

Years ago, I heard one of the assistant general superintendents of a Pentecostal church explain how he learned the importance of praise. When he was seventeen years old, he went to a certain town in the Midwest to hold a youth revival. Well, the pastor was called away to preach a funeral at a church that he had formerly pastored. He had to drive a while to get there, so he couldn't get back overnight.

During the night, one of the pastor's parishioners called because a little child had a high fever and had gone into convulsions. So the pastor's wife awakened the young minister, who was staying in the parsonage with the pastor's family, and they went to pray for the child.

The superintendent said, "Several other people had also gone to pray for the child, but they looked to me because I was the only preacher present. So I anointed the child with oil, laid hands on the child, prayed, and rebuked the devil. I said and did everything I had seen other preachers do, but the child was no better.

"After a while, the pastor's wife began to praise God. One by one, we all picked it up until all of us were praising God. And the convulsions stopped! Later, we were standing around talking when the child went back into another convulsion. We went through the same process again: I anointed the child with oil, laid hands on the child, prayed, and rebuked the devil. Then the pastor's wife began to praise God again. We all joined in. The convulsions stopped, never to return!" You see, the answer came while they were praising God, because that's the kind of atmosphere the Holy Ghost moves in!

9

It was right to pray. Prayer is the first step. But if you wanted to stand on a high platform, just because you took the first step doesn't mean you'd be on the platform. You'd have to take all the other steps too.

The example of Paul and Silas praying and singing praises to God at midnight is not in the Bible just to fill up space. That example is there to inform us and to show us how to gain the victory.

How I Learned About the Power of Praise

You've probably heard me tell my testimony of healing before. I was bedfast for sixteen months, and it would take sixteen months to tell you everything that happened! So I'll refer mostly to the part that's pertinent to what I'm talking about in this chapter—gaining the victory through praise.

Since the time the Lord directed me to teach on faith, I've always emphasized the fact that I acted on my faith after I meditated on Mark 11:23 and 24.

> **MARK 11:23–24**
> **23 For verily I say unto you, That whosoever shall say unto this mountain, Be thou removed, and be thou cast into the sea; and shall not doubt in his heart, but shall believe that those things which he saith shall come to pass; he shall have whatsoever he saith.**
> **24 Therefore I say unto you, What things soever ye desire, when ye pray, believe that ye receive them, and ye shall have them."**

Although I'd been bedfast sixteen months, and the best doctors in America said I had to die, some way or another, I had an inward conviction that my answer was in those verses.

Now my grandfather wasn't really wealthy, but he owned a lot of property. He inquired about putting me on a train and sending me to the great Mayo Clinic in Rochester, Minnesota, to see if they could help me.

But the Mayo Clinic answered back, "One of the doctors on your grandson's case [there were five] is the number one surgeon and one of the foremost physicians in the world. We have him come here every year to teach different surgical techniques. He has told us, 'As far as medical science has any record of, no one in Kenneth Hagin's condition has ever lived past the age of sixteen.'" And four months before my sixteenth birthday, I became totally bedfast. I was going just the way the doctors said I would go.

But, thank God, I got born again, and the Holy Ghost came to live on the inside of me! He was leading me, and I didn't even know it at first. He was talking to me, and I didn't know it. I didn't know you were supposed to listen!

On August 8, 1934, less than two weeks before my sixteenth birthday, I was so helpless that Momma had to bathe me. She left me propped up on two large pillows with the Bible propped up in front of me, opened to Mark 11:23 and 24.

I read those verses again and meditated on them. Then I said, "Lord Jesus, when You were here on earth, You said, *'What things soever ye desire, when ye pray, believe that ye receive them.'* Well, I desire to be healed. I have prayed, and I believe."

Then in tones of kindness and humility, not arrogance, I said, "Lord, if You stood here in the flesh,

11

reached out and took my hand in Yours, looked into my face, and said, 'Son, your problem is you don't believe.' I'd have to say, 'Dear Lord Jesus, that's not true. I *do* believe.'"

When I said that out loud in the room by myself, on the inside of me, in my spirit, I heard these words: "You do believe, all right, as far as you know." You see, Jesus said in John chapter 16 concerning the Holy Spirit, *"Howbeit when he, the Spirit of truth, is come, he will guide you into all truth: for he shall not speak of himself; but whatsoever he shall hear, that shall he speak"* (v. 13). So, thank God, He does speak, doesn't He?

You see, the Holy Spirit didn't say, "Your problem is you don't believe." He said, "You do believe, as far as you know." That meant I didn't know enough. You see, faith is based on knowledge of God's Word. The more you know about the Word, the more faith you'll have. That still small voice of the Holy Spirit went on to say, "You do believe as far as you know, but that last clause goes with that verse." Then He quoted the last part of Mark 11:24.

You see, I'd just been concentrating on three-fourths of Mark 11:24: *"What things soever ye desire, when ye pray, believe that ye receive them . . . ."* But the Holy Spirit reminded me of the last clause, *"and ye shall have them."*

Then I saw it. I don't mean I saw it with my natural eyes. I said, "I see it! I see where I've missed it. I've been trying to get healed first and *then* believe it."

The Bible says that whatsoever you desire, when you pray, you're to believe that you receive, and you'll have what you prayed for. If it's healing you desire, when you pray, believe that you receive healing, and you'll have healing. If it's finances you desire, when you pray, believe that you receive finances, and you'll have finances.

So I saw what I had to do while I was still lying there and hadn't moved a "peg"—while I still hadn't taken a step. You see, from my waist down I was paralyzed. I could see I had a body down there, but I couldn't feel it. Yet while I was still lying there, I had to believe I received healing for the paralysis. While my heart was still not beating right and jumping around like a model-T Ford hitting on one cylinder, I had to believe I received healing for the deformed heart. And I had to believe I received healing for the incurable blood disease the doctors said I had.

I knew it wouldn't take that long, but I said, "I believe I receive my healing. And if I'm still lying here in bed fifty years from now, I'll still be saying the same thing and believing the same thing."

Praise Is an Expression of Your Faith

Well, I've told that part of my testimony again and again. But in teaching on prayer, I was reminded by the Holy Spirit of something. At the very time I was taking the steps I just told you about, I had an inward urge or prompting to praise the Lord.

Now at sixteen years of age, I'd never heard anyone say, "Praise the Lord" or "Glory to God." I'd never heard anyone say, "Hallelujah" or any other kind of praise word. All I'd ever heard anyone say was, "Amen" at

13

the end of a prayer. The pastor might pray before he preached, or he might call on one of the deacons to pray, but no one ever said anything other than, "Amen" when he got through. That's all I'd ever heard, and I had been in church all of my life. Well, saying, "Amen" is not praising God.

But I had an urge to praise God. You see, the Holy Spirit will always lead you and guide you in line with the Word. You may not even know it; I surely didn't know it, but the Holy Spirit knows that prayer and praise go together. He knows that prayer is not going to be effective without praise. I had that inward prompting, that something on the inside of me, urging me to praise God. So I just did it! I began to say out loud, "Praise the Lord! Hallelujah! Glory to God! Thank You, Jesus!"

It sounded strange to me because I'd never heard anyone say anything like that. But I just obeyed that inward urge, saying, "Glory to God! Hallelujah! Praise God, I believe I'm healed! I believe I receive healing!"

I think I must have praised God for ten minutes. Then I heard these words in my spirit: "Now you believe that you are well."

I said, "I certainly do!" Then I heard that still small voice say, "Get up, then! Well people ought to be up at ten o'clock in the morning."

Now tell me, how is a paralyzed person going to get up? But I made the effort. I sort of "draped" myself over the bedpost, with my arms wrapped around it and my knees sagging to within two inches of the floor.

But I said, "I want to announce in the Presence of Almighty God, the Lord Jesus Christ, and the Holy Spirit—and I want to call the devil and all the demon

14

spirits to record—that according to the Word of God, I believe I receive my healing!"

Then I felt something strike me on the top of the head. It felt as though someone was pouring warm honey on me. I could feel it striking my head and then oozing down my face. It went over my body—down my arms, out my hands, and then down to my waist. From my waist down I had no feeling, but I was beginning to have some sensation in my legs. I suppose all the nerves in my legs were reactivated, because for just a few brief seconds, my legs felt as if someone was sticking ten thousand pins in them!

A day or two later, I told someone, "It hurt so bad, I could have cried if it hadn't felt so good!" Now that sounds like a contradiction, but when you don't have any feeling at all, it feels good to feel *anything*! Well, the pain didn't last very long and soon I was standing up straight, glory to God!

Here's what I want you to see: *The answer came while I was praising God.*

—2—
God Inhabits the
Praises of His People

The Bible says, *"But thou* [God] *art holy, O thou that inhabitest the praises of Israel"* (Ps. 22:3). So you could say it this way: "God inhabits the praises of His people."

But if there are no praises, there is nothing for Him to inhabit! Praising God creates an atmosphere for Him to work in. That's why the answer comes while you're praising God. Psalm 22:3 doesn't say, "He inhabits the *prayers* of His people." Yes, God *hears* the prayers of His people, but He *inhabits* their praises!

Now you might be an inhabitant of Jackson, Mississippi. That means you live there. Well, the Bible says that God inhabits the praises of His people. That means that's where He lives!

The Bible also says, *"In the mouth of two or three witnesses shall every word be established"* (2 Cor. 13:1). We've already studied Acts 16:25. Now let's look at another example of how praising God brought about a mighty deliverance.

2 CHRONICLES 20:1-7, 10–12, 14–15
1 It came to pass after this also, that the children of Moab, and the children of Ammon, and with them other beside the Ammonites, came against Jehoshaphat to battle.

17

2 Then there came some that told Jehoshaphat, saying, There cometh a great multitude against thee from beyond the sea on this side Syria; and, behold, they be in Hazazontamar, which is Engedi.

3 And Jehoshaphat feared, and set himself to seek the Lord, and proclaimed a fast throughout all Judah.

4 And Judah gathered themselves together, to ask help of the Lord: even out of all the cities of Judah they came to seek the Lord.

5 And Jehoshaphat stood in the congregation of Judah and Jerusalem, in the house of the Lord, before the new court,

6 And said, O Lord God of our fathers, art not thou God in heaven? and rulest not thou over all the kingdoms of the heathen? and in thine hand is there not power and might, so that none is able to withstand thee?

7 Art not thou our God, who didst drive out the inhabitants of this land before thy people Israel, and gavest it to the seed of Abraham thy friend for ever? . . .

10 And now, behold, the children of Ammon and Moab and mount Seir, whom thou wouldest not let Israel invade, when they came out of the land of Egypt, but they turned from them, and destroyed them not;

11 Behold, I say, how they reward us, to come to cast us out of thy possession, which thou hast given us to inherit.

12 O our God, wilt thou not judge them? for we have no might against this great company that cometh against us; neither know we what to do: but our eyes are upon thee. . . .

14 Then upon Jahaziel the son of Zechariah, the son of Benaiah, the son of Jeiel, the son of Mattaniah, a Levite of the sons of Asaph, came the Spirit of the Lord in the midst of the congregation;

15 And he said, Hearken ye, all Judah, and ye inhab-itants of Jerusalem, and thou king Jehoshaphat, Thus saith the Lord unto you, Be not afraid nor dismayed by reason of this great multitude; for the battle is not yours, but God's.

Although the battle was not the Israelites' battle, but God's, the people still had a part to play. In other words, they didn't just sit down and say, "Well, the battle is the Lord's, so we'll just sit here until He does something." Let's continue reading that passage.

2 CHRONICLES 20:16–20
16 To morrow go ye down against them: behold, they come up by the cliff of Ziz; and ye shall find them at the end of the brook, before the wilderness of Jeruel.
17 Ye shall not need to fight in this battle: set yourselves, stand ye still, and see the salvation [or deliverance] of the Lord with you, O Judah and Jerusalem: fear not, nor be dismayed; to morrow go out against them: for the Lord will be with you.
18 And Jehoshaphat bowed his head with his face to the ground: and all Judah and the inhabitants of Jerusalem fell before the Lord, worshipping the Lord.
19 And the Levites, of the children of the Kohathites, and of the children of the Korhites, stood up to PRAISE THE LORD GOD OF ISRAEL WITH A LOUD VOICE ON HIGH.
20 And they rose early in the morning, and went forth into the wilderness of Tekoa: and as they went forth, Jehoshaphat stood and said, Hear me, O Judah, and ye inhabitants of Jerusalem; Believe in the Lord your God, so shall ye be established; believe his prophets, so shall ye prosper.

Verse 20 is saying that if you don't believe what the prophet said, you won't prosper in it. You have to *believe* the Word of the Lord to benefit from it. Then, as we read in verse 15, you don't sit around and wait for what you're believing for to come to pass. No! You must *act* on the Word!

> **2 CHRONICLES 20:21–22, 24–25**
> 21 And when he [Jehoshaphat] **had consulted with the people, he appointed singers unto the Lord, and that should praise the beauty of holiness, as they went out before the army, and to say, Praise the Lord; for his mercy endureth for ever.**
> 22 And **WHEN THEY BEGAN TO SING AND TO PRAISE, THE LORD SET AMBUSHMENTS AGAINST THE CHILDREN of Ammon, Moab, and mount Seir, WHICH WERE COME AGAINST JUDAH; AND THEY WERE SMITTEN. . . .**
> 24 And **when Judah came toward the watch tower in the wilderness, they looked unto the multitude, and, behold, they were dead bodies fallen to the earth, and none escaped.**
> 25 And **when Jehoshaphat and his people came to take away the spoil of them, they found among them in abundance both riches with the dead bodies, and precious jewels, which they stripped off for themselves, more than they could carry away: and they were three days in gathering of the spoil, it was so much.**

Again, notice the answer came while they were praising God. They had already prayed (vv. 4–12), but the answer, their deliverance, came while they were singing praises unto God. That's what brings God on the scene. God inhabits the praises of His people. That means He's in the praises. *That* means He's *there*! God always comes on the scene when His people are praising Him.

2 CHRONICLES 5:13–14
13 It came even to pass, as the trumpeters and singers were as one, to make one sound to be heard IN PRAISING AND THANKING THE LORD; and when they lifted up their voice [They weren't quiet about it!] with the trumpets and cymbals and instruments of musick, and praised the Lord, saying, For he is good; for his mercy endureth for ever: that then THE HOUSE WAS FILLED WITH A CLOUD, even the house of the Lord;
14 So that the priests could not stand to minister by reason of the cloud: FOR THE GLORY OF THE LORD HAD FILLED THE HOUSE OF GOD.

Notice again that if they hadn't praised God, there would have been nothing for Him to inhabit! (That's the reason He's not in manifestation in most churches.)

In Second Chronicles chapter 5, the Israelites were dedicating Solomon's Temple. The musicians and singers became as one, praising God. When they began to sing and to praise, saying, "The Lord is good, and His mercy endureth forever," the glory of God filled the house of God so that the priests could not stand up to minister!

The glory of God sometimes comes into manifestation as a cloud. I've seen it many times in my services. While we are praising God, I see it over the heads of the people. And the cloud will get "thicker" as we praise Him, because He inhabits the praises of His people! We're going to see this more and more when we move up to greater glory.

—3—

Moving Into Greater Glory

Do you want to move up to a greater glory? Do you want to move up to a higher height, spiritually speaking? I like that first expression, "greater glory." I'll tell you why later in this chapter.

As we were getting ready for *Campmeeting '87*, I was praying about what to minister on, but I couldn't get settled on anything. We always have other speakers, but I usually start off on Monday night. Early on Thursday morning (it was past midnight) before *Campmeeting* started, I woke up and began to pray. I've always done a lot of praying in the nighttime. So I prayed in other tongues for more than three hours.

My book and audio series, *Plans, Purposes, and Pursuits,* came out of that time of prayer. I prayed most of it out in tongues and then interpreted my prayers.

At the end of that time of prayer, I had a vision. I saw the Tulsa Convention Center, where we hold our annual *Campmeeting* and have done so for the last twenty or so years. And Jesus and I were standing about where the ceiling of the building was, looking down on one of the *Campmeeting* services. The auditorium was full of people, and everyone was clapping. Then Jesus turned to me and said, "Clapping is neither praise nor worship."

23

Well, that startled me for a moment. So He went on to explain: "Clapping is *applause*."

Then He illustrated it to me saying, in effect, "If clapping were praise or worship, then people at political rallies are praising and worshipping God when they clap. And people at ball games are worshipping God when they clap. You shouldn't clap for God; you should *reverence* Him."

'Lifting Up Holy Hands'

Someone said, "What about Psalm 47:1, which says, 'clap your hands and shout unto God'"? Well, you can't take one isolated verse of Scripture and build a doctrine on it. That is the only verse in the entire Bible that tells us to clap our hands.

PSALM 47:1
1 [To the chief Musician, A Psalm for the sons of Korah.]
O clap your hands, all ye people; shout unto God with the voice of triumph.

Did you notice to whom this psalm was given? This psalm was given to the chief musician, so we know it's all right to clap while we sing. That is all this verse has reference to. The word "clap," relative to people praising God, is only mentioned in the Bible this one time. But the Book of Psalms alone tells us more than 150 times to praise God. That's because praising God is more important than clapping.

You know, you won't find one other scripture in the entire Old or New Testament that mentions clapping in connection with praising God. No, the Word of God says that our lips should offer praise and thanksgiving to God.

HEBREWS 13:15
15 By him [Jesus] therefore let us offer the sacrifice of praise to God continually, that is, the fruit of our lips giving thanks to his name.

That verse gives us direct instructions to praise the Lord. We also have a New Testament scripture that tells us exactly how to use our hands in worshipping the Lord.

1 TIMOTHY 2:8
8 I will therefore that men pray every where, LIFTING UP HOLY HANDS, without wrath and doubting.

One definition of "prayer" is *communication with God*. When you're praising God, you're certainly communicating with Him, aren't you? So it wouldn't do an injustice to that verse to read it like this: "I will, therefore, that men *praise* every where, lifting up holy hands, without wrath and doubting." This verse tells believers what to do with their hands.

Jesus also said to me, "The world *claps*, but the saints *praise*."

Think about it. You don't see the world lifting up their hands to praise God, do you? So we shouldn't bring the customs of the world into the Church.

Then the Lord said to me, "You've gone as far as you can go [spiritually] under the present circumstances. Tell

My people to quit clapping and start praising. Then they will move up to greater glory."

That's where I got the expression, "greater glory." The way we'll move into God's greater glory is through reverencing the Lord.

Reverencing the Presence of God in Our Midst

If you're a student of history or know something about the history of the Bible, you know the Bible wasn't originally printed with a typewriter or with typesetting equipment. The Hebrew scribes wrote it out by hand. They had such a reverence and respect for God that when they'd come to His Name—and He was known in the Old Testament by a number of different Names—before they'd ever write His Name, they'd stop and take a bath and put on clean clothes.

We've gotten away from showing God the proper respect and reverence that we should. For example, in days gone by, sometimes folks would say, "Let's give God a hand." To me that's unscriptural and irreligious, because it brings God down on a lower level. We shouldn't bring God down on a human level because He's God! He's Holy!

I've also heard people say, "If the President of the United States were here, we'd all stand and give him a hand. Well, One greater than the President is here: *Jesus* is here! So let's stand and give Him a hand." But you don't *applaud* God. That brings Him down on a human level. You're not reverencing God by applauding Him like you would a politician.

We need to learn when to clap and when not to clap. Clapping while we're singing is fine. And when a speaker is introduced, it's all right to applaud and let the speaker know you're glad he or she is there. But I think that when a singer or a choir sings a beautiful, anointed song, instead of applauding them for what they did, we should lift our hands and praise God. If you enjoy the singing, you should say, "Praise God," "Hallelujah," or "Glory to God!" Just praise God and give Him the glory, don't applaud the singers!

Not only that, but when a preacher makes a good point in a sermon or gives a good illustration, don't start clapping, because if the preacher keeps on preaching, some folks will miss what's said. But if you'll start praising God, it will be like saying, "Sic 'em" to a dog! That preacher will take off, because you're flowing with the Holy Spirit when you praise God! But you're out of the flow when you're clapping. Hebrews 13:15 says, *Let us offer the sacrifice of praise to God continually, that is, the fruit of our lips giving thanks to his name.* The fruit of your lips is you *saying* something. So don't clap—open your mouth and praise God!

The problem is we've become "clap happy"! We just clap over anything and everything. That's not good manners, much less good sense. And while I'm on the subject, let me also say that it shows bad manners when people get up and leave a service when the Spirit is moving. It grieves the Holy Ghost, and if we grieve Him, we can't move into the greater glory. We need to learn to flow with the Holy Spirit and return to true praise and worship.

Sixty years ago in our meetings, we had no clapping whatsoever. People praised God. We had a deeper reverence for the things of God than there is today, and we had a deeper move of the Spirit in those days. I believe we're getting back to that. We will have a deeper move of God when we reverence the things of God as we should.

You know, I've been in services where I was giving the interpretation of a tongue or speaking by the spirit of prophecy, and right in the middle of it, someone started clapping and everyone joined in. They didn't hear half of what was said.

If the Holy Ghost is speaking to us through tongues and interpretation or prophecy, we should be quiet and listen. And when it's over, we should lift our hands and praise God for the manifestation of the Holy Ghost.

I've also been in meetings where the Holy Spirit was moving, and the anointing came upon me to minister to certain people. Once I pointed to a woman wearing a pink blouse and by the word of knowledge began to tell her what was wrong with her so I could minister healing to her. But as soon as I spoke to her, everyone started clapping and the anointing lifted from me. Just like a bird sitting on your shoulder, it flew away—the anointing left—because God inhabits the *praises*, not the *clapping*, of His people.

I went away from those meetings weeping, because those folks didn't have enough spiritual discernment to know that they had grieved the Spirit of God. The problem was they weren't reverent enough, they weren't "deep" enough spiritually. They were floating in the soul-ish realm.

That grieves the Holy Spirit, because He's trying to say something and we're not listening. I've seen many a good service ruined because the lack of reverence for God moving in the service grieved the Holy Spirit and He left. The Spirit of God just flat departed, not from me or from anyone else individually, but from the service.

You Have a Responsibility to Flow With the Holy Ghost

One of these days, we are each going to have to stand before God and give an account for what happened in the services we attended. Some people want to put all the responsibility on the preacher. But no one—no preacher, minister, pastor, or teacher—can do any more with a congregation or group of people than they will let him do.

Now you can prove that by Jesus—and He had the Spirit without measure. No other man has ever had the Spirit without measure. And yet Jesus couldn't do a mighty work in His own hometown.

> **MARK 6:5–6**
> **5 And he could there** [in Nazareth] **do no mighty work, save that he laid his hands upon a few sick folk, and healed them.**
> **6 And he marvelled because of their unbelief. . . .**

The Greek translation says, "He laid His hands on a few folks with minor ailments." Those were the only folks He managed to get healed in His hometown. Why? Because of their unbelief.

At the last church I pastored, there was a fellow who wasn't a member of our church, but he visited our church regularly. One day he said to me, "I would sure hate to be in your shoes."

Well, I looked down at my shoes, because I didn't know if he was talking about the pair of shoes I had on or what. (They were the best I could afford in that day, but they didn't look too bad to me.)

So I asked him, "What do you mean you'd 'hate to be in my shoes'? Are you talking about the shoes on my feet? Or do you mean you'd hate to be in my place— married to the woman I'm married to or driving the car I'm driving? What do you mean by that?"

Then a really serious look came on the man's face and he said, "Why, don't you know that you'll have to give an account to God for everything you preach and teach?"

I said, "Don't you know that *you're* going to have to give an account to God for everything that I preach and teach?"

He said, "What! Me!"

I said, "Yes! And I'll prove it to you by the Word." I went over the parable of the sower with him (Mark 4:3–8). I explained that the sower went forth to sow, and since the seed is the Word of God, the sower was a preacher or teacher of God's Word. Then I asked him, "Did you notice that Jesus spent all that time telling that story and He only mentioned the *sower* once? Jesus never said anything about the sower's responsibility. He spent all of His time talking about the *hearer*. He wound up talking about the hearer's responsibility by saying, *'Take heed therefore how ye hear'*" (Luke 8:18)! You see, you're responsible for what you hear.

Of course, ministers are responsible for what they preach and teach, but where does the greater responsibility lie? With the hearer!

My wife and I knew a born again, Spirit-filled, tongue-talking woman who loved to go to church. She never missed a service, because she loved to see God move. She never got in on anything, but she loved to see others get blessed. In one conversation with my wife and I, the woman admitted, "Oh, yes, I love good preaching, but I never pay any attention to it. I just sort of let it go in one ear and out the other."

"Why?" we asked.

"Well," she said, "if I don't know, I won't be held responsible."

But you're held responsible because you heard the Word, whether you know it or not.

Why the Lord Directed Me to Hold Holy Ghost Meetings

It's important that believers be taught how to flow with the Holy Spirit. The Lord told me several years ago that there was a move of the Spirit that would be lost to this generation if it wasn't taught. So He told me to hold different kinds of services—Holy Ghost Meetings.

When I asked the Lord "What is a Holy Ghost Meeting?" He said, "Number one, in a Holy Ghost Meeting, the Word of God is preached and/or taught. Number two, the Holy Ghost is leading, guiding, and directing in manifestation and demonstration. Number three, the needs of the people are met and the joy of the Lord is manifested."

You see, every meeting has a different purpose. For instance, the purpose of a prayer meeting is to pray. The focus of an evangelistic crusade is to get folks saved and filled with the Holy Ghost. And in a healing rally, people come to receive healing—and so forth. Of course, all those things can happen in *any* meeting, but there ought to be a specific purpose every time we meet.

So since 1993, I have been holding Holy Ghost Meetings, endeavoring to teach people how to flow supernaturally with the Holy Ghost. In our Holy Ghost Meetings, the main emphasis is on the Person and manifestations of the Holy Ghost, but the Word of God always has the preeminence. In other words, we put God's Word *first*, and supernatural signs and demonstrations *follow* the preaching or teaching of the Word (Mark 16:20).

As the Spirit Wills

We know from Scripture that spiritual gifts and manifestations operate as the Spirit wills: *"But all these worketh that one and the selfsame Spirit, DIVIDING TO EVERY MAN SEVERALLY AS HE WILL"* (1 Cor. 12:11). We need to realize that one person can't do it all. God uses different people in different ways. In the Holy Ghost Meetings that I hold, I don't have to preach every service. We hear from different ones as the Lord directs. It's not a one-man show—God will use whoever He wants to use.

I've talked with some men who were around during the early days of the Pentecostal Movement in the United States. They told me that many times in some of the camp meetings and different meetings, they'd have a teacher speaking in the morning service and an evangelist speaking at night. They left the afternoon service open for visiting speakers or anyone the leaders felt led to call on. The leaders would ask, "Who has the message?"

Smith Wigglesworth was a British preacher and when he first came to America, no one knew him. He attended an Assemblies of God camp meeting in the Bay Area of California, and they had him speak one afternoon. The leaders of the meeting saw that the anointing was upon him, so they turned all the night services over to him. They said, "He's got a message we need to hear."

They already had an evangelist there who was supposed to speak every night, but he didn't get his feelings hurt when they turned the services over to Brother Wigglesworth. If the Holy Ghost wanted to move that way, let Him!

Whatever the Lord wants to do is fine with me. Whomever He wants to use is fine with me, because some are especially anointed in some areas.

In the days of the healing revival here in America, from 1947 to 1958, nearly every healing evangelist in America advertised in *The Voice of Healing* magazine.

We'd have a Voice of Healing Convention every year around Thanksgiving.

In 1954, we met in Philadelphia. Several ministers were talking together. One minister said that he had great success in ministering to people who were deaf, or deaf and mute. Practically everyone he ministered to would get healed. Another minister said, "I have never gotten a deaf person healed. But if people have something wrong with their eyes, blind or whatever, most every time they get healed."

On another occasion, Brother F.F. Bosworth, who wrote *Christ the Healer*, told me, "In one healing service, I gave an altar call and said, 'If you have anything wrong with your ears—whether you're deaf, deaf and mute, or even if you've been operated on and your eardrum has been removed—I want you to come forward.' Nineteen people came and they were all healed! I don't know why, but it always works that way."

Well, I didn't know why either, but I got in the Word and found out! Brother Bosworth got deaf and mute people healed because that's where his gift was. You see, the gifts of the Spirit are manifested as the *Spirit* wills. Did you ever notice what the Bible said about Philip in the eighth chapter of the Book of Acts?

> ACTS 8:5–7
> 5 Then Philip went down to the city of Samaria, and preached Christ unto them.
> 6 And the people with one accord gave heed unto those things which Philip spake, hearing and seeing the miracles which he did.
> 7 For unclean spirits, crying with loud voice, came out of many that were possessed with them: and

many taken with palsies, and that were lame, were healed.

The healings under Philip's ministry were in a certain category, because that's where he was gifted. Verse 6 says, "the people gave heed to the things Philip said, hearing and seeing the miracles which *he* did."

First Corinthians 12:9 says there are "gifts of healing." In the Greek translation of this verse, both words are plural: *"gifts* of *healings."* According to the Word of God, Jesus is the only One who had the Spirit without measure. When He was here on earth, His physical body was the only Body of Christ on the earth. Now *we* are the Body of Christ. He's the Head and the Church is the Body.

JOHN 3:34
34 For he [Jesus] whom God hath sent speaketh the words of God: for God giveth not the Spirit by measure unto him.

I believe that the entire Body of Christ, collectively, has the Spirit without measure, but you and I, as individuals, don't. We only have the Spirit by measure. That's the reason we need to get in meetings and services where the Holy Ghost is moving, because *"the manifestation of the Spirit is given to every man to profit withal"* (1 Cor. 12:7).

Give the Holy Ghost Free Rein

Believers have a lot to do with how the Spirit of God moves in a service. We need to create an atmosphere in which the Holy Ghost is free to move.

1 CORINTHIANS 3:16
**16 Know ye not that ye are the temple of God, and
that the Spirit of God dwelleth in you?**

The *Amplified Bible* says, "Do you not discern and understand that you [the whole church at Corinth] are God's temple (His sanctuary), and that God's Spirit has His permanent dwelling in you [to be at home in you, collectively as a church and also individually]?"

You see, God's Spirit dwells in the body of believers and that's where He'll manifest Himself. Ministering to the Lord with a body of believers creates opportunities for gifts of the Spirit to operate.

For example, in January 1953, I was preaching at Brother Lewis' church in Tyler, Texas. One day he asked, "Brother Hagin, do you remember my niece." I told him I did, because the last church I'd pastored was in a town close to Tyler.

"Well," Brother Lewis said, "she has cancer in both lungs. We feed her six times a day and she's still losing weight. A few months ago, I put her through the cancer clinic here and after they ran the tests, they told us that she had cancer in her left lung."

They wanted to remove the lung immediately before it could spread any further. Now that was 1953 and we didn't have all the sophisticated medical equipment we have today.

Brother Lewis continued, "We didn't just accept that report. I put her through another clinic, and they said the same thing. When my niece spoke up and said that she would like to pray for one week about having

36

surgery, the doctor said, "We believe in prayer, but in a week, the cancer can spread too far."

But she took the time and prayed. At the end of the week she said, "No. I'm not going to be operated on. I'll just trust God to heal me and if I die, I die." She should have said, "I'll trust God and live." Many weeks passed and the cancer spread to her right lung. The doctors said it was too late for an operation even if she had wanted one.

She was bedfast now, so they got her out of bed and brought her to one of my services. I'd only minister to the sick on Tuesday and Friday nights. They'd keep her in a side room where she could hear the message over a speaker. Then they'd bring her in and put her in the healing line.

I had laid hands on her four times in two weeks but nothing happened. On Tuesday night of the third week, they got her out of bed again and brought her to the service. This time when I laid hands on her for healing there was a manifestation of the Spirit. Suddenly, it was like a white cloud enveloped me. I had my eyes wide open, but I couldn't see the crowd—they were gone, disappeared. I just saw myself and this young woman standing in the cloud. In the Old Testament, the glory of God was very often manifested in cloud form when the people were praising God.

I saw a little monkey-like creature, it was actually a demon, clinging to her body over her left lung (where the cancer started). I commanded that evil spirit to leave her in the Name of Jesus, and he said, "Well, I know I have to go if you say so, but I sure don't want to."

I said, "Leave her," and he fell on the floor and laid there shaking like a little pup you'd whipped. And I said, "Not only must you leave her body, but you must also leave these premises." He ran down the aisle and out the door of the church, and the woman was healed! She was twenty-three years old and had been saved since she was eight, but she had never been filled with the Holy Spirit. Well, she lifted her hands and started praising God and began to speak with tongues.

That same week, they took her back to the doctors, and she requested new X-rays and tests of her lungs. Now she didn't look any better, so the doctors told her that more tests were not necessary. But she insisted, so they ran every test they could.

The doctors said, "We don't understand it. The cancer has disappeared. What happened?"

She told them exactly what had happened, that it was God's power that had made her completely whole. Those doctors said they would give her a written affidavit stating that she had cancer of the lungs, but now it was gone!

The point I'm making is that if *I* had been the one doing the healing, I would have done so the first time I prayed for her rather than the fifth time. You see, the operation of the Spirit is not something that we can control, it operates as God wills. But we can create the type of atmosphere in which the Holy Spirit is free to move.

Many times the Holy Spirit is hindered from moving as He wants to because believers fail to reverence the Presence of God in their midst. Moving into God's greater glory has to do with learning to flow with the Holy Spirit.

We must learn to be more sensitive to the Spirit of God. If we'll reverence the Holy Spirit, we'll have more manifestations of the Holy Spirit.

In the churches that my wife and I pastored, we had constant revival. People were saved, filled with the Holy Spirit, and healed on a regular basis. You could hardly come to our meetings without receiving, praise God. Our congregations learned to follow the Holy Spirit and flow with Him.

Yet in many churches today, when someone answers an altar call, people will start clapping. Thank God that people are being saved. But we're not to applaud them—we're to thank God. We're to give Him the praise and the glory.

When you're clapping, you're not flowing with the Spirit. You're trying to worship God in the natural. And some folks have gotten in such a habit of clapping that when you try to get them to praise God, they don't know how.

I know that's why the Lord told me that the Body of Christ had gone as far as we could go, spiritually. But when we quit clapping and start praising God, we will move up to *greater glory*! Now you'll get all kinds of responses to that statement, but the Word of God is clear on the matter.

Acts 16:25 doesn't say, "At midnight Paul and Silas prayed, began to clap, and the prisoners heard them." No! That verse never said a single word about clapping. It said that Paul and Silas prayed and *sang praises* unto God. God inhabits the praises of His people.

And Second Chronicles 20:22 doesn't say, "When the children of Israel began to sing and to *clap*, the Lord set ambushments against the enemy." No! When they began to sing and to *praise*, the Lord set ambushments against their enemies.

You see, they'd already prayed; the answer came while they were singing praises. The victory was won while they were singing praises. Or to put it another way, the glory came while they were singing praises. Whatever the answer is that you need, expect it to come when you praise God.

When God's people praise Him, God does something! That's when God's power is manifested and the enemy is defeated in people's lives! That's why it's so important for us to understand when it is appropriate to clap and when we should praise God. When we learn to praise and worship the Lord in the right way, we will experience a deeper move of the Holy Spirit in our midst. I challenge you to praise God instead of clapping. I guarantee you'll experience a deeper move of the Spirit.

More than fifty years ago the Lord said to me: "If you'll do what I tell you to do, there will be a restoration of what you saw back then." Sometimes you'll hear me refer to some of the spectacular, supernatural manifestations of the power of God that we experienced in the past. And in recent years, the Lord said to me, "Not only will there be a *restoration* of those things, but then there will be a *multiplicity*." They'll be multiplied. Glory to God!

So don't grieve the Holy Spirit by clapping at the wrong times. Understand what the Holy Spirit is saying and doing and learn to flow with Him. Unless we do this, there's a move of the Spirit that will be lost to this generation. I don't believe it will be lost, because I believe we're going to move on up from glory to *greater glory*!

"What should I do with my life?"

If you've been asking yourself this question, **RHEMA BIBLE TRAINING COLLEGE is a good place to come and find out.** RBTC will build a solid biblical foundation in you that will carry you through—wherever life takes you.

The Benefits:

◆ Training at *the* **top Spirit-filled Bible school**

◆ Teaching based on steadfast faith in God's Word

◆ Unique two-year core program specially designed to **grow** you as a believer, help you **recognize the voice of God**, and equip you to **live successfully**

◆ Optional **specialized training** in the third- and fourth-year program of your choice: Biblical Studies, Helps Ministry, Itinerant Ministry, Pastoral Ministry, Student Ministries, Worship, World Missions, and General Extended Studies

◆ **Accredited** with Transworld Accrediting Commission International

◆ Worldwide **ministry opportunities**— while you're in school

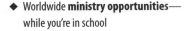

Apply today!
1-888-28-FAITH (1-888-283-2484)
rbtc.org

Rhema Bible Training College admits students of any race, color, or ethnic origin.
OFFER CODE—BKORD:PRMDRBTC

Always on.

For the latest news and information on products, media, podcasts, study resources, and special offers, visit us online 24 hours a day.

rhema.org